P9-AQU-214

Wild Life™ LOL!

Grizzly Bears

Don't call me Teddy!

SCHOLASTIC

Library of Congress Cataloging-in-Publication Data
Title: Grizzly bears
Description: New York, NY: Children's Press, an imprint of Scholastic Inc., 2020. | Series: Wild Life LOL! | Includes index.
Identifiers: LCCN 2019006051| ISBN 9780531240380 (library binding) | ISBN 9780531234914 (paperback)
Subjects: LCSH: Grizzly bear—Juvenile literature.
Classification: LCC QL737.C27 G758 2020 | DDC 599.784—dc23

Produced by Spooky Cheetah Press

Design by Anna Tunick Tabachnik

Contributing Jokester: J. E. Bright

No part of this publication may be reproduced in whole or in part, or stored in a retrieval system, or transmitted in any form
or by any means, electronic, mechanical, photocopying, recording, or otherwise, without written permission of the publisher.
For information regarding permission, write to Scholastic Inc., Attention: Permissions Department, Scholastic Inc., 557 Broadway,
New York, NY 10012.
© 2020 Scholastic Inc.

All rights reserved. Published in 2019 by Children's Press, an imprint of Scholastic Inc.

Printed in Heshan, China 62

SCHOLASTIC, CHILDREN'S PRESS, WILD LIFE LOL!™, and associated logos are trademarks and/or registered trademarks of
Scholastic Inc.

1 2 3 4 5 6 7 8 9 10 R 29 28 27 26 25 24 23 22 21 20

Scholastic Inc., 557 Broadway, New York, NY 10012.

Photographs ©: cover, spine: Evan Meyer/Shutterstock; cover speech bubbles and throughout: pijama6/iStockphoto; cover speech
bubbles and throughout: Astarina/Shutterstock; back cover: Scott E Read/Shutterstock; 1 and throughout: John Delapp/Design Pics/
Getty Images; 3 top: Raycroft/Minden Pictures; 3 bottom: George Sanker/Minden Pictures; 4: Paul Sawer/Minden Pictures;
5 girl silo: Nowik Sylwia/Shutterstock; 5 bear silo: oorka/Shutterstock; 8-9: Naphat Photography/Getty Images; 10-11: Ron Sanford/
Science Source; 12-13: Pete Ryan/Getty Images; 13 center: McPHOTO/picture alliance/blickwinkel/M/Newscom; 14: Ronan Donovan/
Getty Images; 15 top left: Whitney Cranshaw/Colorado State University/Bugwood.org; 15 top right: Laura Romin & Larry Dalton/Alamy
Images; 15 bottom left: Drew Rush/Getty Images; 15 bottom right: Jordana Meilleur/Alamy Images; 16: Michael Jones/Getty Images;
17 left: Juniors Bildarchiv/age fotostock; 17 right: David Arment/iStockphoto; 18-19: MyLoupe/Universal Images Group/Getty Images;
20: Leonard Lee Rue III/Science Source; 21 left: CSP_ricochet64/age fotostock; 21 right: Ron Niebrugge/Alamy Images; 22-23: Richard
Wear/Getty Images; 25 left: John Weinstein/Field Museum Library/Getty Images; 25 right: George Sanker/Minden Pictures; 26 left:
Joel Bennett/Getty Images; 26 right: Gunter Marx/Alamy Images; 27 left: George Sanker/Minden Pictures; 27 right: Klein-Hubert/
Kimballstock; 28 top: KeithBinns/iStockphoto; 28 bottom left: taden/iStockphoto; 28 bottom right: George Sanker/Minden Pictures;
29 top: Suzi Eszterhas/Minden Pictures; 29 bottom: Iakov Filimonov/Shutterstock; 30 map: Jim McMahon/Mapman®; 30 bottom: Mark
Raycroft/Minden Pictures; 31 top: Ingram Publishing/Superstock, Inc.; 32: Paul Sawer/Minden Pictures.

TABLE OF CONTENTS

Meet the Mighty Grizzly.......................... 4

A Grizzly Bear's Body 6

Wait! This Is Not a Grizzly...................... 8

Home on the Range.............................. 10

Smell Ya Later! 12

Who's Hungry?................................... 14

A Long Winter's Nap............................ 16

Starting a Family................................18

Welcome, Cubs!................................. 20

Growing Up Grizzly 22

Grizzlies from the Past......................24

Grizzlies and People........................... 26

Grizzly Cousins 28

The Wild Life........... 30

Index 32

About This Book 32

This looks BEAR-y interesting!

MEET THE
MIGHTY GRIZZLY

Are you ready to be amazed and amused? Keep reading! This book is BEAR-y entertaining!

Hey! Wanna see me build a den with my BEAR hands?

LOL!
How do bears keep their dens cool?
BEAR-conditioning.

At a Glance

Where do they live? → Grizzlies live only in North America—in the northern United States and Canada.

What do they do? → Grizzlies spend a lot of time eating to prepare for their long winter sleep.

What do they eat? → Almost anything, including berries, grass, roots, insects, and young elk and moose.

What do they look like? → Grizzlies have large bodies, long claws, and a hump of muscle on their backs.

How big are they? →

Check this out:

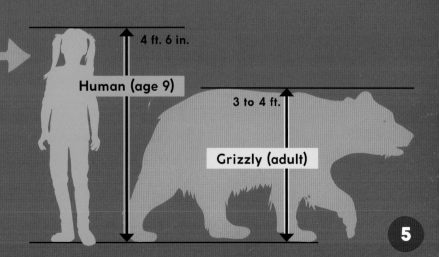

4 ft. 6 in.

Human (age 9)

3 to 4 ft.

Grizzly (adult)

A GRIZZLY BEAR'S BODY

The grizzly bear is one of the largest meat-eaters in North America. It has a massive body.

I Only *Look* Old
Fur on the grizzly's shoulders and back has white tips. That's where the name "grizzly" comes from.

LOL!
What do you call bears with no ears? "B!"

Hey, Big Guy!
An adult male grizzly weighs about 600 pounds.

Flex!
The hump on a grizzly's back is made of muscle. It makes this bear a dynamite digger.

Nail-ed It!
A grizzly's claws are always out. The bear uses them to uncover food, dig dens, and kill prey.

THAT'S EXTREME!
A grizzly's claws can be longer than your hand.

WAIT! THIS IS NOT A GRIZZLY

Not all brown bears are grizzly bears! There are many types of brown bears. Grizzlies are just one type. Here's how to tell the difference.

Hey, are you a grizzly?

Bear Essentials
All grizzlies are brown bears, but not all brown bears are grizzlies. Other brown bears are named for where they live.

salmon

WACKY FACT: The largest brown bear may weigh about 400 pounds more than a grizzly.

Little Brother
Grizzlies are sort of small . . . compared to other brown bears, that is.

Alaskan brown bear

Nope. I'm an Alaskan brown bear. And that makes YOU my lunch!

Landlubbers
Grizzlies live inland, not near **coasts**. Coastal bears hunt salmon. Grizzlies don't.

coasts: lands that lie along the sea

HOME ON THE RANGE

A grizzly bear's neighborhood is its home range.

Table for One

Grizzlies mostly live alone—except for when a female bear has her cubs with her.

Where Should I Eat?

The size of a bear's range depends on how much food is around. If food is hard to find, a bear will need to cover a lot of ground to eat its fill.

Nice Neighborhood!

A grizzly's range can include lots of different **habitats**. The bears might explore forests and mountains, as well as large, open grassy fields.

habitats: places where a plant or an animal makes its home

THAT'S EXTREME!
A male grizzly's range can cover an area larger than New York City.

WACKY FACT:
Some grizzlies' fur is so light that it looks blond instead of brown.

I hope nobody else found my favorite blueberry bush!

SMELL YA LATER!

Whew! You need a bath, stinky!

Bears have the best sense of smell of any animal.

THAT'S EXTREME!
Grizzly bears can smell food from miles away—even if the food is underwater!

Better Than a Map

Grizzlies use smell to figure out where they are. By smelling, they can tell what is nearby and what is far away.

WACKY FACT:
Grizzlies also leave deep scratches and bite marks on the trees they rub against.

I'll just let everyone know I stopped by.

I Know You!

Grizzlies also recognize each other by smell. Sometimes a grizzly will rub against a tree to leave its scent behind. This lets other bears know the grizzly was there.

WHO'S HUNGRY?

Grizzlies need to add fat to their bodies before winter. They eat A LOT of insects, roots, and berries. They also hunt young animals, such as elk and moose.

THAT'S EXTREME!
Grizzlies in Yellowstone National Park may eat 40,000 moths in a day!

WACKY FACT:
A grizzly can eat 90 pounds of food in one day. That's like eating 200 hamburgers!

I'll even eat other animals' leftovers!

remains of a bison

moths

roots

I'm really DIGGING these roots!

These are some of a grizzly's favorite meals.

squirrels

berries

A LONG WINTER'S NAP

During the long, cold winter, little food is available. Grizzlies go into a deep sleep called **hibernation**. They need to find the perfect spot to rest. Here's how they do that.

I feel a major yawn coming on.

1

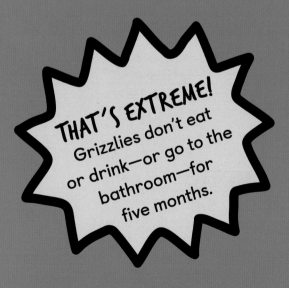

THAT'S EXTREME!
Grizzlies don't eat or drink—or go to the bathroom—for five months.

As it roams across
its range, a grizzly is always on the lookout for a safe, warm spot to sleep the winter away.

hibernation: a long period of sleep during cold weather

WACKY FACT:
It takes a grizzly three to seven days to dig a den.

Look, a perfect fit!

2

3

The bear might find a natural den, like a small opening in the side of a hill. The bear will try it out. If the den is comfortable, the bear will spend the winter there.

If the grizzly doesn't find a natural den, it will dig a little cave for itself.

STARTING A FAMILY

In early summer, male grizzly bears start looking for females that are ready to **mate**.

1

Something's in the Air

A male's sense of smell tells him if a female is ready to mate.

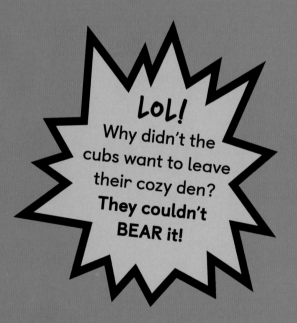

LOL!
Why didn't the cubs want to leave their cozy den? They couldn't **BEAR** it!

mate: to join together to have babies

2

Getting Ready

In fall, the female bear prepares her den, where she will give birth. The male wanders off on his own again.

3

Hello, Baby Bears!

The female gives birth to her babies, called cubs, during hibernation.

WELCOME, CUBS!

Grizzlies can have from one to four cubs at a time. Because they are **mammals**, the cubs' first food is their mother's milk.

I love to cuddle with my sis!

1

LOL!
What do you call a bear with no teeth?
A gummy bear!

Too Cute!

Newborn cubs weigh only about 1 pound. They have no fur and can't see yet. The cubs begin drinking milk right away while their mother sleeps.

Just a Sip

The cubs begin eating solid food when they are a few months old. But their mother continues to feed them milk for two to three years.

Getting Big!

The cubs grow fast! By the time spring comes, they will weigh at least 13 pounds. The cubs will be fully grown by the time they are five years old.

mammals: animals that produce milk to feed their young

GROWING UP GRIZZLY

Grizzly mothers keep a very close watch over their cubs. The family stays together until the cubs are two or three years old.

Learning
The cubs watch their mother to learn how to find food and hunt.

I'm no teddy bear. You DO NOT want to cuddle with me!

Playing
Cubs spend a lot of time playing. They run around and climb on logs. They wrestle.

WACKY FACT:
Female bears are called sows. Males are boars.

All Grown Up!
When the cubs are ready to be on their own, their mother is ready to mate again.

GRIZZLIES FROM THE PAST

Bears have been living on Earth for millions of years. Scientists know this because they have found **fossils** like this one.

Who Are You Calling "Short"?!
This is a skeleton of a short-faced bear. It lived in North America more than a million years ago.

THAT'S EXTREME!
Even on all fours, the short-faced bear was taller than most fifth graders!

One Big Bear!
When standing on its hind legs, the short-faced bear was 12 feet tall.

fossils: plants or animals from millions of years ago preserved as rock

GRIZZLIES AND PEOPLE

Bears and people have a long history together.

This Native American blanket has a bear design.

Pre-1800s

For thousands of years, Native Americans lived in peace with grizzly bears. Many native people saw the bears as sacred and treated them with respect.

1800s

European settlers moved into the American West and began hunting grizzlies. In less than 200 years, almost 50,000 bears were killed.

1970s

Bears play a big role in nature. For example, they spread seeds in their poop that grow into plants. People realized they should be protected.

Today

The U.S. government passed laws that made it illegal to hunt bears. Today about 30,000 grizzlies live in Alaska and about 1,500 in the rest of the country.

Grizzly Cousins

Bears are related to other meat-eating animals, like tigers and raccoons. Here are the grizzly's closest cousins. They are all bears.

I'm the most common bear in North America.

American black bear

You can recognize me by the whitish fur on my chest.

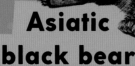

Asiatic black bear

It's easy to see we're related!

The Wild Life

In the early 1970s, grizzlies were on the brink of **extinction**. Look at this map of the world. The areas in red show where grizzlies live today. We want grizzlies to continue having habitats to live in. Otherwise, one day there might not be any red left on this map.

Canada

United States

extinction: when no member of a species is left alive

What Can You Do?

1 If you visit or live in an area where grizzlies live, leave them alone! You may be able to tell if they are around by looking for their tracks.

2 Learn more about the main threats to grizzly bears: loss of habitat, trouble with humans, and climate change. Look for organizations that continue to work to protect grizzlies and their habitats, such as the Yellowstone to Yukon Conservation Initiative (Y2Y).

3 Speak up! Tell everyone what you learned about grizzlies. The more people know about how important grizzlies are, the more people will want to protect them.

INDEX

brown bears 8–9

claws...7

cubs.......... 10, 19, 20–21, 22–23

food............................9, 12, 14–15

fur.................................... 6, 11, 20

habitats.....................................10

hibernation 16–17, 19

hump 7

range. 10–11, 16

rub trees..................................... 13

short-faced bear 24–25

size 6

smell...............................12–13, 18

starting a family 18–19

weight 6, 8

ABOUT THIS BOOK

This book is a laugh-out-loud early-grade adaptation of *Grizzly Bears* by H. W. Poole. *Grizzly Bears* was originally published by Scholastic as part of its Nature's Children series in 2019.

I can't BEAR to say goodbye!